FREELANCE EXPERT

LEARNING THE SECRET OF GETTING FREELANCING SUCCESS!

Maryalice Swiney-Zoë

Jungle Boogie Ink

Copyright © 2017 by Maryalice Swiney-Zoë.

All rights reserved. No part of this publication may be reproduced, distributed or transmitted in any form or by any means, including photocopying, recording, or other electronic or mechanical methods, without the prior written permission of the publisher, except in the case of brief quotations embodied in critical reviews and certain other noncommercial uses permitted by copyright law. For permission requests, write to the publisher, addressed "Attention: Permissions Coordinator," at the address below.

Maryalice Swiney=Zoë/Jungle Boogie Ink

Street Address

3894 Crenshaw Blvd. Unit 561495, Los Angeles, CA 90056.

www.60degreesapphiremagazine.com

Ordering Information:

Quantity sales. Special discounts are available on quantity purchases by corporations, associations, and others. For details, contact the "Special Sales Department" at the address above.

Freelance Expert: Learning the Secret of Getting Freelancing Success! / Maryalice Swiney-Zoë. —1st ed.

ISBN-13:978-1976277825

Contents

Introduction 6
Potential 7
Drawbacks 7
    Taxes 7
    Interruptions 8
    Instability 9
    Lack of Benefits 9
    Writing 10
    Design 11
    Artwork 12
    Voiceovers 13
    Video Editing & Creation 13
    Other Ideas 14
Finding Work 15
    Your Portfolio 15
Fiverr 16
    Webmaster Forums 18

Freelance Websites..19

Writing Websites 20

Conclusion 21

Resources 22

Copyright © All rights reserved worldwide.

YOUR RIGHTS: This book is restricted to your personal use only. It does not come with any other rights.

LEGAL DISCLAIMER: This book is protected by international copyright law and may not be copied, reproduced, given away, or used to create derivative works without the publisher's expressed permission. The publisher retains full copyrights to this book.

The author has made every reasonable effort to be as accurate and complete as possible in the creation of this book and to ensure that the information provided is free from errors; however, the author/publisher/ reseller assumes no responsibility for errors, omissions, or contrary interpretation of the subject matter herein and does not warrant or represent at any time that the contents within are accurate due to the rapidly changing nature of the Internet.

Any perceived slights of specific persons, peoples, or organizations are unintentional.

The purpose of this book is to educate and there are no guarantees of income, sales or results implied. The publisher/author/reseller can therefore not be held accountable for any poor results you may attain when implementing the techniques or when following any guidelines set out for you in this book.

Any product, website, and company names mentioned in this report are the trademarks or copyright properties of their respective owners. The author/publisher/reseller are not associated or affiliated with them in any way. Nor does the referred product, website, and company names sponsor, endorse, or approve this product.

COMPENSATION DISCLOSURE: Unless otherwise expressly stated, you should assume that the links contained in this book may be affiliate links and either the author/publisher/reseller will earn commission if you click on them and buy the product/service mentioned in this book. However, the author/publisher/reseller disclaim any liability that may result from your involvement with any such websites/products. You should perform due diligence before buying mentioned products or services.

This constitutes the entire license agreement. Any disputes or terms not discussed in this agreement are at the sole discretion of the publisher.

A good way to create a portfolio is by setting up a website...

CHAPTER 1

Introduction

Freelancing is one of the best ways to earn money, because there's such a high demand for services such as graphics design, website design, and writing. Sure, there is also a lot of competition to deliver these services, but it's a lot easier than you probably think to set yourself apart from the competition.

 A lot of people prefer freelancing, because you don't have to be tied down to a certain location at a certain time, and you have the potential to earn a lot more money for the time you spend working than you would if you were working for someone else.

There are a lot of benefits to working on a freelance basis, but there are also some drawbacks, and we'll discuss a few of those so you can make a more informed decision as to whether or not you'd like to give it a try.

In this guide, we're going to take a look at some of the more common ways you can earn money freelancing, as well as some lesser-known methods and places you can find work.

We'll also take a look at some of the ins and outs of freelancing to help you decide if it's really right for you.

CHAPTER 2

Potential Drawbacks

You probably already know most of the positive aspects of freelancing, such as the potential to make more money and the ability to work in your underwear at home or even on the beach in Tahiti. Pretty cool, right? But there are a few drawbacks to consider, as well.

Let's take a look at a few of the drawbacks that might make you reconsider freelancing. (Remember, you can always do freelance work while employed traditionally if you're not ready to leap right into fulltime freelancing. In fact, that's usually the best idea!)

Taxes

Ugh, taxes. It's something you don't think much about when you work a normal job, because your taxes get taken out of your check and the only time you really have to worry about it is tax season when you have to file your taxes.

But when you're a freelancer, you have to worry about taxes all the time. You have to save money from every payment to cover taxes, and it really hurts when you have to write out that check to Uncle Sam, because it all comes in one lump sum—unless you pay your taxes quarterly.

Taxes for a freelancer can be pretty complicated, so if you aren't a tax professional, you'll probably want to hire one to help you—at least in the beginning.

A good accountant will be able to teach you the basics of recordkeeping for tax purposes, and they'll also help you when it comes to filing your taxes, so it's a great idea to get a consultation with one as soon as possible.

Interruptions

Interruptions are huge productivity killers in any workplace, but if you work from home you'll soon discover it's much worse. People think that because you work at home, you'll be free to talk to them, hang out with them, do them favors, etc. as if you didn't work at all. And if you protest, they get offended as if you don't want to talk to them at all.

People who have never worked from home will never truly grasp what it's like, so there's really no easy way to help them understand that they can't just expect you to have the ability to drop whatever you're doing at any moment for them.

For this reason, it's a very good idea to turn off your cell phone and go into a room with a closed door while you work. Ideally, you might even want to rent office space so you can have more privacy while you work. This may not always be possible, but if you can, office space in many areas is remarkably affordable.

Instability

Finding work as a freelancer isn't guaranteed, and you may find the lack of a guaranteed paycheck is too much to deal with. Because work is so unstable, especially in the beginning, many freelancers work a full-time or part-time job to supplement their income.

You can increase your chances of finding work consistently by putting yourself in as many freelance marketplaces as possible, presenting a professional portfolio of work, and seeking references and testimonials that may help others choose you over their competition.

Lack of Benefits

One huge thing that is a deal-breaker for a lot of potential freelancers is the lack of any benefits such as retirement and health insurance. While a lot of jobs don't offer such benefits, either, most people don't end up staying at those jobs for very long.

Health insurance for the self-employed is outrageously expensive, but if your income is relatively low you can qualify for Medicaid, or at least a reduced price on your health insurance.

Retirement is a huge issue, and it's important to start saving early. Self-employed individuals should start an IRA (Individual Retirement Account) as early as possible and contribute the maximum amount possible to be sure they have money available for retirement, because they won't be paying money into Social Security and thus cannot collect any when they retire.

Remember, there are drawbacks to everything—even traditional jobs. Freelancing may not be for everyone, but for others, it's the only thing that makes them happy.

CHAPTER 3

Services

First, we're going to talk about some of the different services you might be interested in offering as a freelancer. Some of these will probably be obvious, but since you might not immediately think of all of them.

There are so many different services you could potentially offer to clients, and you can make money with whatever you find most interesting and have the most talent and ability to do.

Writing

Writing is the first thing most people think of when it comes to freelancing, because it's the one thing that doesn't take a lot of natural talent or technical training to do. Most people have enough of a grasp of basic English spelling, grammar and punctuation to take at least basic writing jobs.

In fact, some freelance designers or programmers do writing work on the side to supplement their income in between design jobs.

Because writing has a fairly low barrier to entry, it's also highly competitive and doesn't pay as much as some other types of freelancing. A simple article can pay as low as $1.50, but more complex jobs, especially if they need to be very high in quality, can pay significantly more.

There are many different types of writing you can do as a freelancer.

For example:

- Blog posts and articles
- Short reports
- Non-fiction e-books
- Fiction (books, stories, poetry, etc.)

Different types of work pay different amounts, but technical writing and fiction writing (such as ghostwriting romance books for authors) can pay quite a lot.

Design

Design requires a little bit more technical ability than writing, but if you have the aptitude for it and the experience, you can make good money doing all types of freelance graphic work.

At the basic end of the design spectrum are things like advertising banners and book covers. These require only a graphics program like Photoshop or GIMP, some stock photos, and a decent level of talent.

At the higher end are projects like posters, as well as projects that require some more technical ability like designing websites and user interfaces for apps and programs.

Here are some ideas for the types of graphics you can create:

- Book covers for authors
- Advertising banners
- Posters and flyers
- Websites and blogs
- Logos

If you want to get work as a designer, it's extremely important to create a good portfolio with examples of what you can do. If you have never done a particular type of work before, create a few examples for your portfolio, even if they are fictional. (For example, create a cover for a book that doesn't exist, or create your own version of the cover of a popular book.)

You could also offer to do work for people for free in the beginning to build your portfolio, but keep in mind that even if you're offering free work, some people will want to see what you can do before they commit to working with you so they don't waste your time and theirs if they end up not liking what you produce.

Artwork

If you're a talented artist in any medium, there's a great opportunity for you to earn money with that talent. Gone are the days when the only way an artist could make money was by selling original paintings. These days, artists have a lot of possibilities for earning!

- Portraits and caricatures
- Other commissions
- Book cover art

- Children's book illustration
- Art for apps and video games
- T-shirts, posters, and other items to sell
- Prints of artwork (possibly framed for hanging on the wall)

These are just a few ideas of ways you can make money as a freelance artist. There is a nearly endless number of other ways!

Voiceovers

If you have a good voice and don't have a very thick accent of any kind, you might want to consider doing voiceover work.

Voiceover work is simple and requires very little technical knowledge. As long as you can read well, speak clearly, and perform basic computer functions, you can offer your voice for videos, audiobooks, and other projects.

The only things you'll really need for voiceover work are:

- A decent computer
- Audio processing software
- A good microphone (a must)
- A location good for recording (such as a closet)

Video Editing & Creation

Video editing is a more advanced skill that requires a little more technical knowledge and ability, but if you have the talent for it, you can make very good money creating videos and editing those that other people have created.

Video is quickly taking over text and photos as the media of choice online, and many individuals and companies are using them for a variety of promotional purposes.

Videos can be used for publicity, such as when celebrities post them on Facebook or Instagram. They can be used to promote something specific, such as when a restaurant posts a video of their newest dish and a limited time price promotion. Or they could be used in many other ways to publicize, promote, and sell.

Videos don't have to be extremely complex. In fact, they don't necessarily even have to contain any video. They could be just slideshows of photos or graphics with text, music, or voiceovers. Sometimes that format is even more effective than traditional videos.

Other Ideas

There are many other ways you can make money from home or on a freelance basis. Some of them include:

- Keyword research
- Photo editing Translation
- Photography
- Programming and app creation
- Selling crafts online
- Selling used items online

These are just a few ideas. What's your greatest talent? What's the thing you enjoy doing most? Chances are, you can find a way to make money with it!

CHAPTER 3

Finding Work

Finding work is generally the most difficult part of freelancing. In almost every area (writing, design, etc.) there is a ton of competition. And by "a ton", I mean thousands upon thousands of people competing for the same jobs.

But don't feel hopeless! The fact is, most of the competition is severely unprepared for the available jobs and many people just don't know how to get them.

In this section, you're going to learn about some of the various ways to find work as a freelancer, and how you can stand out from the competition in order to get more jobs and command a higher rate for your work.

Your Portfolio

One of the most important elements of being a successful freelancer is having a stellar portfolio available that shows your best work. (Be sure to ask every client before you use their project in your portfolio.

There are many reasons a client might not want their project to appear, and you don't want to have a client upset because you used their project without permission.)

A good way to create a portfolio is by setting up a website with WordPress. WordPress is much easier for the average user to use than standard HTML and CSS. Of course, if you're more comfortable with HTML and CSS, you can use that instead. WordPress just makes website setup a lot quicker and easier for those who aren't well-versed in HTML and CSS.

Your portfolio should feature some of your best work, as well as contact information and testimonials. Testimonials should ideally include a photo of the person giving it, as well as a link to their website or contact information in case potential clients would like to verify the testimonial.

So what if you don't have any work to show?

The best thing you can do is either make some samples that are meant simply to show your talent, or just take a few simple projects for free or at a heavy discount in order to build your portfolio.

Don't use a free hosting service for your portfolio unless you are able to have your own domain name for it. It's just not professional to host your site on a free server, and you may run into downtime issues that could cost your business. Hosting is only about $10 per month,

Fiverr

One of the quickest and easiest ways to find work is through Fiverr and other similar sites.

- http://www.fiverr.com

Don't think you must charge only $5 for your work. As the name of the site implies, most items are priced at $5, but you can also have upcharges that can increase the amount of money you receive for the work.

For example, you could write articles at 300 words for $5, and offer 600-word articles for $10 and 1,200-word articles for $15. People would order the 300-word article and add the upgrade to receive a longer article.

There are also some alternatives to Fiverr you can check out:

- http://www.fiverup.com
- http://www.gigbucks.com
- http://www.zeerk.com
- http://market.source-wave.com/
- http://www.seoclerks.com
- http://www.microworkers.com

One of the most popular places for finding work as an artist is at DeviantArt.com (http://www.deviantart.com). You can create an artist portfolio on the site, including different galleries with different types of artwork, and contact information to let people who are interested in your work contact you.

Other sites you can use to sell artwork, crafts, and other items include:

- http://www.art.com

- http://www.amazon.com

- http://www.ebay.com

- http://www.cafepress.com

- http://www.etsy.com

- http://www.fineartamerica.com

Webmaster Forums

Webmaster forums can be a fantastic source of freelance work of all kinds. They often have thousands of active members daily, and many of them need services such as the ones we've discussed on a regular basis. Make a good name for yourself on these forums and you could end up with more work than you can handle!

Here are some of the more popular forums:

- http://forums.digitalpoint.com

- http://www.warriorforum.com

- http://www.webmasterworld.com

- http://www.sitepoint.com

- http://www.webhostingtalk.com

- http://forums.seochat.com

Freelance Websites

The most obvious place to find work is through various freelance websites. Many of these are very well known, and get a tremendous amount of traffic. Yes, there is a lot of competition, but you can stand out from the competition in many ways.

First, you can make sure your profile and portfolio are the best they can be. Make sure you have plenty of quality examples of your work so people feel more assured that you can deliver what you say you will.

Next, you can work hard to complete jobs quickly to build feedback so people will trust you more than others. This is key, because people are rarely patient when it comes to getting work done.

Finally, you can compete on price by trying to be the lowest bidder, at least in the beginning. As you're building feedback and a portfolio, you shouldn't worry too much about money. Just take the jobs that fit your skillset at the best price you can get. You can charge more later, once you have built your business.

Here are some of the most popular freelance websites where you can try to find work:

- http://www.upwork.com (formerly Odesk)
- http://www.toptal.com
- http://www.elance.com
- http://www.freelancer.com

- http://www.guru.com

- http://www.peopleperhour.com

- http://www.ifreelance.com

- http://www.99designs.com (design contests)

Writing Websites

Writing gig websites don't typically pay much, but they're great for finding work in between regular jobs, and they help you build valuable writing experience you can use later.

Here are some popular sites:

- http://www.freelancewritinggigs.com

- http://www.textbroker.com

- http://www.wordgigs.com

- http://www.skyword.com

- http://www.copypress.com

- http://www.iwriter.com

- http://www.constant-content.com

Conclusion

Freelancing is not for everyone. You have to deal with taxes, the potential instability of income, constant interruptions, having to motivate yourself, and more. Not everyone can deal with these things. But if you can, you can make more money and have more freedom than almost any job could provide.

Best of all, you don't need some ridiculously expensive college degree. Employers often expect you to have a degree, even if you're far more talented and experienced than other candidates. Why would you go into debt with student loans only to end up making less working for someone else than you could working as a freelancer?

You must treat it like a regular job if you want to be successful. Create a regular work schedule and stick to it as much as you can. Try to minimize distractions. And be sure to let your friends and family know that when you're working, you can't be interrupted.

Don't expect to make a fortune right away. Like any type of business, it takes a while before you start seeing good results, because you need time to build a reputation and get into the swing of things fully. But once you do, the sky's the limit!

Resources

Here are links to some of the resources found in this guide.

Freelance Marketplaces:

- http://www.fiverr.com
- http://www.fiverup.com
- http://www.gigbucks.com
- http://www.zeerk.com
- http://market.source-wave.com/
- http://www.seoclerks.com
- http://www.microworkers.com

Art Marketplaces:

- http://www.deviantart.com
- http://www.art.com
- http://www.amazon.com
- http://www.ebay.com
- http://www.cafepress.com
- http://www.etsy.com
- http://www.fineartamerica.com

Webmaster Forums:

- http://forums.digitalpoint.com
- http://www.warriorforum.com
- http://www.webmasterworld.com
- http://www.sitepoint.com
- http://www.webhostingtalk.com
- http://forums.seochat.com

Freelance Websites:

- http://www.upwork.com (formerly Odesk)
- http://www.toptal.com
- http://www.elance.com
- http://www.freelancer.com
- http://www.guru.com
- http://www.peopleperhour.com
- http://www.ifreelance.com
- http://www.99designs.com (design contests)

Writing Websites:

- http://www.freelancewritinggigs.com
- http://www.textbroker.com

- http://www.wordgigs.com

- http://www.skyword.com

- http://www.copypress.com

- http://www.iwriter.com

- http://www.constant-content.com

- http://mariansweb.com

Freelance Expert

*Remember, there are drawbacks to everything—
even traditional jobs*

Maryalice Swiney-Zoë

Best of luck with your new freelance business!